WORSHIP IN THE WILDERNESS

Let Praise Lead the Way (A Christian Devotional Collaboration)

DEVOTIONAL COLLABORATIONS   MICHAEL LACEY
CASSIDY POE   BECKY SIMS   TANYA DUFFEY
JACKIE PERSEGHETTI   AMI LOPER   LEENA J.
ERIN WATSON MOHR   N C R   TANJA TUOVINEN
IRISH GAMBITO   SHARON HAZEL
MIRANDA J. CHIVERS   LAUREN ROSKILLY
KATIE ARTHUR   ROBERT KAPEN

D1445313

Contents

Preface

Worship in the Wilderness is a collection of devotions that can be read daily throughout the month. This collection is formed with various authors around the world. You may notice different spellings or styles such as "Savior" versus "Saviour". We celebrate the international feel and have retained author styles.

The viewpoints of each author do not reflect those of everyone involved. We differ on some theological issues, but our goal is to come together—despite those differences—to share messages that challenge us to be faithful through troubled times.

DISCLAIMER: if you have any issues with the theologies (which do vary slightly), or any devos in particular, please reach out to those authors directly. Each of us are passionate about the Word of God, and if we are risking blasphemy or causing damage in any way, we WANT to know. God's word is holy, and it deserves our best. Each writer is allowed to share their beliefs in a judgment-free way.

However, one core belief holds true for all of us: salvation (and thus eternity in heaven with God) is available to all who call upon the name of Jesus, as outlined in John 14:6 and John 3:16, of course.

May the real stories from these real people reflect the real God and help you receive the favor of forgiveness in your life.

You are not alone. You are loved. You are here for a reason.

Godspeed,

-Michael Lacey, Story-Builds.com (and the Devo Writers Collaborations group)

Special Thanks

A portion of the proceeds from each Devo Writers Collaboration goes to a related charity after production and marketing costs are met. By purchasing this devotional collection, you are supporting victims of COVID-19 and others who need our help through the Christian Relief Fund. Click on the link if you'd like to support them directly!

So, we collectively shout, "THANK YOU!" for your 'donation', and we have faith you will draw nearer to God through these heartfelt writings.

Introduction

We are called to worship at all times: on mountaintops, in the valleys, in the land of promise, and in the wilderness. For you, the wilderness may be a financial drought, or maybe physical, emotional, or spiritual. These seasons are not usually the direct result of sin but rather a God-ordained time for you to learn more about His character and will for your life.

You are not alone. People throughout the Bible have gone through wilderness seasons: Job, Hagar and Ishmael, Moses, the Israelites after Egypt, Elijah, possibly John the Baptist, Paul, Jesus, many of whom were righteous and blameless. Yet they still showed us how to grow closer to God through it all.

In the wilderness, we learn so much about God's provision and our lack of offering to Him. He doesn't need anything yet He desires us; in fact, He requests our hearts, souls, strength, and minds. In the wilderness, we realize how much we need Him, how much He already provides, and how little we have to bring. However, what we have to bring that please Him is our praise, our worship to the King over all, the Creator of everything.

We must confront the wild, the natural, the devil and the Spirit, the opposition to our preferred way of life and the temptation to go (back to) a life of sin. Through the danger and deliverance, wilderness and wastelands, and restoration and revelation, seek solitude for the sake of self-discovery and divine discovery, encounters with God, and the promised land of His presence.

The Greek word for "wilderness" is eremos (or eremia), which like the Hebrew translations, also means "an isolated place."

As we walk through lonely paths we feel no one else has traveled, we begin to see little trails of grace. We see how Christ has gone before us and experienced everything we ever will. And through it all, He gives us all we ever need through His presence. He turns our tragedies into melodies, pain into praise, and (worry, anguish, wilderness,) into worship.

Let your seasons of wilderness refresh and renew, let them purify you and grind the world out so that what remains is a sacrifice honorable to God.

One thing stays true: praising God makes ways where there seem to be no ways. *It's time to praise through 'til breakthrough*.

Take time on a daily basis to go through these devotionals and lean into God's direction for your life personally. Allow these real stories from real people remind you of our very real God.

And when you've gone through this collection, go deeper by grabbing one of the other books in the series and also by tapping some of your favorite writer's links. We write because we are called to, but mostly we want to help. And many of our writers have incredible resources, writings, teachings, and offerings to help you through your own journey!

> *Lastly, if you're a writer—or even have an inclination to join something like this—go to DevoWriters.com to learn more about what we do and why.*

ONE

Free from Shackles

MICHAEL LACEY

"Everlasting
Your light will shine when all else fades
Never ending
Your glory goes beyond all fame
And the cry of my heart
Is to bring you praise
From the inside out."
—"From the Inside Out" by Hillsong Worship,
lyrics by Joel Houston

The song begins. A guitar plucks out a riff I love that tells me my favorite song is being played. Several emotions flood in, memories of previous worship experiences and times God has spoken to me through these words.

Something sparks in me...

"Should I raise my hands?"

I open an eye to peak and see no one else in the room with their arms up. "Maybe when it gets to the big part near the end?" I decide and close my eyes, fighting the urge to sway for some reason.

As the chorus moves into a soaring bridge, I shout sing the words...and peak around again. Still no one is raising their hands. But I want to. More than that, I know I should—a glimpse of obedience before I know what obedience is. There's something on the inside wanting to be evident on the outside, the deep in me calling out to the deep of God.

"Let's do this slowly."

I lift my hands past my pockets and hold them out like I'm waiting for a gift or maybe offering one. We're only at the second verse, still plenty of time. My wrists are surprisingly heavy, like they're shackled with marine-grade chains attached. The higher I lift, the more thick links I pull off the ground, and the harder it gets. *"What will people think? Especially if I'm the only one doing it?"*

But I can't help it. I want my God to know I worship Him. It's in the words I'm singing, to raise my hands, and in the Word I've been reading. I see it all over the Psalms how people praise with such fervor. Why wouldn't I do the same? My integrity won't let me keep my hands down, and my God deserves my unashamed worship, regardless of what others may think!

The big singing moment is nearly over, so I'm about to lose my chance to truly express myself in worship...like last week or even through the last song. I won't miss my chance to show my love and adoration to God in the sight of men, not again!

I thrust my hands into the air as high as they can go. The shackles break and the chains fall. The momentum of my obedience pulls my body off the ground until I'm on my tippy-toes, stretching everything I have to glorify and honor my King, my Savior, my God.

"And immediately all the doors were opened, and everyone's bonds were unfastened." —Acts 16:26 (ESV)

Lord, King of my heart, help me to be praise You openly. Pass Your courage to me so I can worship boldly. Break the chains of those around me as we worship You together. Let my fervor be an example and an inspiration, but let them see Your power at work through it all, not mine.

Michael is responsible for putting these collections together and produces books through Story Builds Creative (Story-Builds.com). He helps writers get their life-changing words into the world on a budget! Get your free writing resource guide at DevoWriters.com to get started!

Michael writes fiction under the pen name M. Lacey. Get some of his stories and books at fiction. michaellacey.me. Coming from the rich writing heritage of Mississippi, he believes in the power of words to inspire and encourage. It is a lifelong calling to put pen to paper (or fingertips to keys) for him, and he doesn't take it lightly.

Finally, Michael is a singer/songwriter and worship leader who is always looking to collaborate and co-write. Find out more (and get some free music) at michaellaceymusic.com.

His goal is to spend as much time with his family as possible, especially while his children are young. Jobs and money come and go, but time only passes. If you'd like to support him in any way, reach out or join his mailing lists to get all of his newest content.

michaellacey.me | Story-Builds.com | DevoWriters.com
Devo Profile: https://amzn.to/3iGe5AO (free journal
now available)
Fiction Profile: https://amzn.to/3odupdg (2 free books
up now!)

TWO

Worship in the Wilderness

MICHAEL LACEY

"When lonely meets the only One, and chaos
finds a path.
From my flesh to the supernatural clearing of my
past,
I will sing. I'll worship in the wilderness.
When wind and rain and fire hits every part of
who I am,
I will worship.
Where sin and pain and lies exist, I'll rest in
Your arms.
I know where the quiet is, in the Savior's song."

—"Worship in the Wilderness", lyrics by
Michael Lacey

Finding your way to worship can be daunting. You'll
sometimes feel stranded, alone, vulnerable. When you
step out of a place of comfort, your old boundaries are
gone. New ones await, but you can't see them yet. It's a
wild and wonderful world of exploration and challenge.

If you've never done this, it's not too late. If you want to worship as the Lord wants you to, then you'll always be exploring and seeking Him out. I don't think any of us are doing it right, not completely. But I know that moving closer to Him is always the answer.

When you are in that wilderness or some barbaric place, you can always find refuge in the Lord; this is a grace that He extends to you when you need Him most. You can rest in the Savior's song, the reminder of that great sacrifice because of the Lord's faithful and everlasting love.

> "Thus says the Lord: 'The people who survived the sword found grace in the wilderness; when Israel sought for rest, the Lord appeared to him from far away. I have loved you with an everlasting love; therefore I have continued my faithfulness to you.'"

—Jeremiah 31:2-3

God, I ask for Your guidance as I traverse wilderness and wastelands. I don't need to see the end, just show me where next to place my feet. And when I can't walk, carry me. I trust You are taking me somewhere I could never get on my own, to a place of true communion with You.

Michael is a worship leader in north Mississippi, and this devo (the next devo) is an excerpt from Michael's book for worshipers and worship leaders called *As We Fight: A Weekly Guide through the Warfare of Worship*. It's a great gift for worship leaders and has been used as a group study as well.

THREE

The Warfare of Worship

MICHAEL LACEY

". . . he appointed those who were to sing to the Lord and praise him in holy attire, as they went before the army, and say, "Give thanks to the Lord for his steadfast love endures forever...And when they began to sing and praise, the Lord set an ambush against the men of Ammon, Moab, and Mount Seir, who had come against Judah, so that they were routed. For the men of Ammon and Moab rose against the inhabitants of Mount Seir, devoting them to destruction, and when they had made an end of the inhabitants of Seir, they all helped to destroy one another." —2 Chronicles 20: 21-23 (ESV)

Worship is a word that covers a lot of ground. It is often in reference to the singing and musical portion of a church service or personal devotion time. It can also mean everything you do while breathing on this earth. In whichever capacity, worship is warfare. *These battles are the collision of God's will, man's will, and the enemy's will, each one demanding worship in one way or another, while only One is truly worthy of it.*

In 2 Chronicles, Jehoshaphat feared men that were coming against him for battle. He sought the Lord and followed His command by doing what seemed insane. He sent the singers first into battle. God's ways are bigger than ours; they must be for something this crazy to be commanded!

In this passage, we see that the singing of, to, and for God *sent the enemy running!* It's amazing to see the way today's services are structured after this pattern of worship: praising God through song and music as the first charge of battle. God has powerful plans in music and worship towards Himself. He has shown us throughout time that He is capable of more than we can imagine. *What men may see as insanity is often what God uses to accomplish His goals.*

In the scriptures, we see this battle cry often: "Give thanks to the Lord, for His steadfast love endures forever." When we look to the enemy, other people, things of this earth, or even ourselves, we can easily lose hope. The tasks look more daunting, spirits are waning, the battle weighs heavily, and the enemy appears immovable. When we look to the Lord, however, we see victory already. We see that His burden is light because it is not something we carry alone. We have God Himself on our side. Or more correctly, we are on His side, the winning side.

This is an excerpt from *As We Fight: A Weekly Guide through the Warfare of Worship.*

"Do not be afraid and do not be dismayed at this great horde, for the battle is not yours but God's . . . You will not need to fight in this battle. Stand firm, hold your position, and see the salvation of the Lord on your behalf, O Judah and Jerusalem.' Do not be afraid and do not be dismayed. Tomorrow go out against them, and the Lord will be with you." —2 Chronicles 20:15, 17 (ESV)

FOUR

How God Desires Worship (7 Hebrew Words, Part 1)

MICHAEL LACEY

"Let them praise (halal) his name with dancing and make music to him with timbrel and harp." —Psalm 149:3

You read that right, let's break out the timbrels! What, you don't have one of those? Maybe the word "tambourine" is more familiar? Don't worry, I'm not suggesting you bring one of those to church next time. The basic point here is to use percussive and rhythmic instruments to praise.

I used to read these kinds of verses and think, *"Sure, someone can do that—the they should—but not me. I'll worship a different way."*

Now, I wonder where I ever got that idea! How many times have you heard or said something like, "I'm not comfortable worshiping like that...?? Since when did 'comfort' become synonymous with our faith or even with church? Where is that in the Bible? Show me a verse that says, "worship/serve the way you feel."

I can't find it, but what I can find are examples of worship. More than that, I find imperative *commands* for worship. Praise and worship are commands, imperative, like saying, "sit" or "stand". "Worship, praise!" And more than that, the Hebrew language—which is what the Psalms were written in—has several words, or commands, for 'worship' and 'praise'.

You may know about the four Greek words for English love: Philia, Agape, Eros, and Storge...but did you know there are also SEVEN Hebrew words for praise as it's used throughout the Old Testament?

The primary Hebrew word for worship is 'shachah', meaning bow down or worship, depending on the context. One of my favorite words for worship is the Greek word, 'proskuneo'. It calls us to kneel before our God. "Proskuneo" means "to kiss" as in to kiss the hand of a superior. It is commonly associated with bowing down or lying prostrate on the ground with the idea of kissing the ground before someone. Some scholars believe the word actually is derived from the idea of a dog licking its masters hand. The idea is to show profound reverence and submission.

Here is a quick overview of the seven Hebrew words—or as I like to say, commands—of worship:

1. <u>Yadah</u>: worship with extended hands, shooting an arrow or throwing a stone, shoot hands into the air. Your affection and desire to show your love to the Lord surpassed all else and you raise your hands.

With my eyes closed, in a moment of expression and obedience, I once threw my hands into the air at the same time someone was walking in front of me. I hit my best friend's mom in the face while worshiping, knocked her glasses clean off.

Here are some more reasons to raise your hands while worshiping:

- victory: a natural response around the globe is to raise hands when something has been won.
- surrender: raised hands makes your vulnerable and is a universal sign of surrender.
- a child running up to his father: one of my favorite pictures, I imagine my child running up to me with arms held high. He or she doesn't have to say a word or make a request; I already know what he and she wants, to be lifted up and held.

2. Halal (like hallelujah): to boast rave shine celebrate to be clamorously foolish. Ps 149:3 with dancing and music. Jewish wedding, dancing man, Laughing from the depths of his soul because two people are coming together who he loves.

I think of my response to seeing my kids excel or just being there to support them. I said I'd never be the one to shout and carry on like my dad did, but now my wife has to hold me back when one of my sons steps onto any stage. Now I know what it means to them to have that support and to me to have no regrets as I celebrate them like it's the last chance.

(Continued)

God, help me not to wait until the next worship experience to put into place these pleasing expressions of praise to You. Right now, wherever I am, I will bow down or raise my hands to You or speak, even shout, Your name. You are worthy! You are good! I praise You!

FIVE

7 Hebrew Words, Part 2

MICHAEL LACEY

"I will not be afraid, I will render praises (towdah) to You." —Psalms 56:12

Worship is often described as a feeling, but it is so important to have true understanding of what it means to worship God. That's why these words are so powerful. Each one gives us insight to our God, what He desires, and the freedom He offers us in our expression of praise to Him.

3. Towdah: an extension of the hand, thanksgiving for things not yet received, a confession, a sacrifice of praise. "I don't worry, I Worship." When things were out of control, move your focus to the one who controls it. Believing when everything you see is challenging you to doubt.

4. Tehillah: a hymn, a song of praise, a new song, a spontaneous song. Ps 22:3

5. Zamar: to make music, to celebrate in song and music, to touch strings or parts of a musical instrument. Music is more powerful than we even understand. It was created to be a conduit to access the presence of God. There's a flower that only opens to the specific chirp of a certain bird.

6. Barak: to kneel, to bless God as an act of adoration, to praise, salute, thank. Wherever the King would go, their eyes were fixed on him. Not how was the Worship, how was your worship.

7. Shabach: to address in a loud tone, to shout, to commend, glory, and triumph. Ps. 117:1 (praise Halal, then praise shabach). A song becomes an anthem, it becomes a holy roar.

Again, these are commands, not suggestions. Our comfort is never more important than His commands. This day may be the day God sets you free. When the moment is set apart for you to worship and praise our great God, lean into one or more of these words. Trust His word and be obedient. Be like David in Psalm 150 with ecstatic and enthused praise when he said he would become even more undignified than this.

Though you may read/hear differently (perhaps even in this book), worship is not for us, not primarily; it's for God. He has served us with His grace more than enough. Why should we take from worship. We are blessing Him with beautiful praise. And when we do that, when we are obediently stepping into His will, He does fulfill us. Then, we do get something for ourselves, but that's not why we do it. That's not where we start.

"Rejoice in the Lord, you righteous ones; praise from the upright is beautiful." —Psalms 33:1 (CSB)

Lord over all, give me guidance and wisdom on how best to worship You, not by what I'm comfortable with but in the way You desire to be worshiped. Teach me what it means to truly worship You for You and not for myself. Lead me and embolden me to be unashamed to the point of foolishness if that's what it looks like to be Your child. I value You and our relationship more than anything this world can offer.

For a deeper dive into these 7 Hebrew words, check out the book *Holy Roar*.

SIX

Suffering as an Invitation to Worship

CASSIDY POE

"I have said these things to you, that in me you may have peace. In the world you will have tribulation. But take heart; I have overcome the world." —John 16:33 (ESV)

"Beloved, do not be surprised at the fiery trial when it comes upon you to test you, as though something strange were happening to you. But rejoice insofar as you share Christ's sufferings, that you may also rejoice and be glad when his glory is revealed." —1 Peter 4:12-13 (ESV)

Suffering. The word itself begs us to turn and run in the opposite direction. But still, as a byproduct of our human condition, we find ourselves in difficult, heart breaking, and life changing circumstances that leave us with a lot of questions and a lot of pain.

10 years ago, I began having mysterious episodes where I collapse and have temporary paralysis in my arms and legs followed by seizures. My then 14 year old self

thought I would go to the doctor and get an answer that would lead to allowing me to resume my life as a normal teenager. However, many doctors, many tests, misdiagnosis', and over six years later, I was finally diagnosed with a rare, incurable genetic disorder. I've seen many bedridden days, many isolated and lonely days.

My body, my spirit, and my heart were tired and weary from a decade of suffering. Truly, the last thing that I wanted to do was pour our worship, rejoicing, and gladness in the middle of my physical and emotional pain. It seemed pointless if my circumstances were not going to change outside of the complete and total healing of the Lord - and He is the one who, after all, had not reached down and done the very thing I have prayed for and believed for.

I remember one day early in my search for answers, I came home from yet another doctor's appointment where the testing came back normal. I walked into the appointment hopeful and walked out disappointed and shattered. Still no answers. I walked into my home and something washed over me where I had to immediately go sit at the piano and play any worship song that I could. I'm not an excellent or classically trained pianist and there were a significant amount of tears that hit the keys, but at that point, I had to make a decision on what my response was going to be; even if my circumstances never changed.

I could take the lack of answers and choose to be angry and withdrawn from everyone; especially the Lord. Or I could pour my heart out and relent into the love of the one who truly has all the answers, even when my doctors didn't.

Something in me shifted. I had to come to the point that if all that I could do was lay in my bed, it was going to be to the glory and honor of Jesus. If my entire being in this world was boiled down to not walking, and hardly being able to get upright; if all I had was the struggle, I was going to let that struggle be an anthem of praise.

Because here is the thing, if we believe God is sovereign and we believe that He deeply loves us, we can trust the wisdom and the love of the Lord that sees fit to allow us to go through deep waters. It is this deep knowledge about the character of God that enables us to worship and praise; even in the middle of our deepest struggles.

> *Father God, thank you so much for who you are. Thank you for your love and for your sovereignty. I know that my struggle and my suffering are not a surprise to you. But right now, I make the decision to lift up a shout of worship. Even in my tears, even in my pain, even as I stand at the edge of the unknown, you are still good and I choose to praise you. Thank you that when I pass through the deep waters, you are with me. In Jesus' name, Amen.*

After over a decade of chronic illness, it is Cassidy's mission to help others who are going through difficult seasons find and put their ultimate hope in Jesus. Cassidy runs an online ministry where she works to equip women with resources to deepen their faith, and also uses her platform to share other women's stories of how God showed up in the middle of their hardest and most difficult circumstances. Her website is a place for women to come, be encouraged, and find community. Learn more and get involved at:

www.cassidysheart.com

SEVEN

Worship as a Demonstration of Trust

CASSIDY POE

"And he said, "Abba, Father, all things are possible for you. Remove this cup from me. Yet not what I will, but what you will." —Mark 14:36 (ESV)

"Trust in the Lord with all your heart and do not lean on your own understanding. In all your ways acknowledge him, and he will make straight your paths." —Proverbs 3:5-6 (ESV)

In the dictionary, worship is defined as showing reverence and adoration for a deity. As Christians, this has so many possible different forms. Songs, playing music, praying, and submitting to the Lord are all forms of worship. There are a number of calls to worship and so many beautiful examples in Scripture of what worship can look like. Perhaps one of my favorite examples of worship can be found in the Gospels. In Mark 14:36, we see Jesus praying in the Garden of Gethsemane knowing that His betrayal, torture, and murder were imminent. In this verse, there are a couple of powerful things that I want us to look at.

At the very beginning of His prayer, Jesus first acknowledges who God is. He recognizes Him as Father and Jesus further acknowledges the power and ability of God to make another way. Jesus makes His request known to His Father, and then ends by acknowledging God's sovereignty over what was about to unfold; even if His prayer to make a different way was answered with a, "no". Jesus begins his prayer with worship and reverence; even though He knew what He was about to endure. And He ended His prayer with submitting in trust to whatever God had planned.

Something that I find so moving about worship is that we get to step into our struggle with our eyes fixed on the one who is able to move in a way that we could not. When faced with incredibly difficult struggles, we can easily become overwhelmed by our inability to change our circumstances. Here, we see Jesus choosing to face the biggest struggle of His human life with first focusing on the power and ability of God. What a powerful example!

When we zoom in and look at our own individual lives, we might not have the knowledge of what is going to happen tomorrow, but we can make the decision to begin with trusting in the character, love, and sovereignty of God, no matter what. When we shift our focus to the unchanging character of God, we are moved to respond in worship. Worship is a declaration of trust that says, "Lord, even though I don't understand and even though I don't know what will happen tomorrow, I will cling to you, hope in you, and believe your promises are true."

Lord, I come before you as Jesus did and I acknowledge that Abba, Father, all things are possible with you. You are God, you are sovereign, you are good. I raise my worship up to you and declare that no matter what tomorrow holds, no matter what is in the cup that you give to me, I will trust you. I will declare your goodness. I will hold fast to your promises and your truth. Thank you, God, for all that you do on my behalf. In Jesus' name, Amen.

EIGHT

Worship is a Weapon

CASSIDY POE

"Having received this order, he put them into the inner prison and fastened their feet in the stocks. About midnight Paul and Silas were praying and singing hymns to God, and the prisoners were listening to them, and suddenly there was a great earthquake, so that the foundations of the prison were shaken. And immediately all the doors were opened, and everyone's bonds were unfastened." — Acts 16:24-26 (ESV)

The clock had long passed 12am and my tired eyes seemed to drill holes into the pitch black ceiling above as sleep evaded me. After multiple seizures and some difficult days, my body was exhausted and my spirit was weary. Somewhere in those early morning hours, I began to sleepily mediate on Psalm 23, working through it line by line in my mind and examining everything it had to teach me about God's provision and character. Unexpectedly, tears began to flow down my cheeks as I sat upright in my bed and began to pray the verses out loud. I resolved in that moment that I wasn't going to stop until I had met with the Lord. I wasn't going to stop until I could lay down in peace. I wielded the only weapons I knew to be powerful enough; worship and the Word of God.

I sang the verses, I cried over the verses, I prayed the verses. I needed my posture to be one of worship because I was being consumed and overwhelmed. Me telling you this isn't to make me seem super-spiritual. Rather, I want you to understand that in those early hours, I was drowning in fear, self-doubt, and discouragement. But Jesus! He steps in and changes everything. God has graciously given us the innate desire to worship (or idolize) the things and people we adore. And when we focus our worship on Him, things start to shift in our heart.

Worship allows us to recenter our attention on Him. It is a weapon that allows us to remove our fixation from our own weaknesses and struggles and instead lock eyes onto the creator of the earth. He is the artist of every sunrise, the one who has immeasurable power with which He used to resurrect Jesus from the grave! Worship allows us to walk in and embody the victory Jesus purchased for us, no matter what our current circumstances are.

Paul and Silas understood this concept better than anyone. As they were put into prison and their feet shackled, the two men were praying and singing songs to God in the midnight hours. Scripture tells us that, "Suddenly, there was a great earthquake, so that the foundations of the prison were shaken. And immediately all the doors were opened, and everyone's bonds were unfastened" (Acts 16:26, ESV). In response to their worship, God broke their chains and paved the way for the jailer to come to know Him.

And you know what? I truly believe with everything inside me that God is still in the business of breaking chains in the midnight hours. Chains of guilt. Chains of shame. Chains of fear. Chains of discouragement. Chains of loneliness. And on and on. Let us wield our God-given weapon of worship and watch as He shows up in a way that only He can!

Father God, I worship you. I adore you. You are Holy and powerful. Thank you, God, that you are a chain-breaker and that you hear our desperate pleas and our worship in the midnight hours of life. You see us and you hear us. I place my focus on you and ask that you come and move in my life in a way that only you can. I ask that you move on my behalf to heal, restore, and redeem. No matter what you allow me to walk through, I trust and I praise you because you are good and there is none like you. In your precious name, Amen.

NINE

Keep Praising with Joy

TANJA TUOVINEN

"You, dear children, are from God and have overcome them, because the One who is in you is greater than the one who is in the world. They are from the world and therefore speak from the viewpoint of the world, and the world listens to them. We are from God, and whoever knows God listens to us; but whoever is not from God does not listen to us. This is how we recognize the Spirit of truth and the spirit of falsehood." —1 John 4:4-6

In July 2020, I had surgery at the hospital, it was during the pandemic year and there were restrictions in place because of COVID. I remember feeling sad because when I was admitted to the hospital, I was told that I would only be allowed a limited number of visitors and visiting hours would only be two hours. It made me feel lonely and isolated, and the feeling that I would be thrown somewhere to the unknown by myself and would I ever be back? I didn't look fantastic after the surgery, and it didn't help me feel better.

My visitor limitation wasn't as bad as I thought it would be, as I was able to have my parents and a good friend come. I decided to do video chats with my friends and have phone calls. Also, one of my friends had said on Sunday that she would be able to visit me as she worked in the hospital. She became my bonus visitor, as the head nurse, she was allowed to come. When she arrived, it was one of those afternoons where I was waiting and waiting for a hospital cup of coffee. My friend surprised me with her presence, smile, and a Starbucks coffee, bottled water, mints, and cookies.

The feeling of loneliness was real for me as I entered the hospital, but even though I'm weak and only human, I have the strength of the Lord. The joy of the Lord is our strength, even in hard moments, we can be strong enough to overcome trials, temptations, or tribulations because greater is He who lives in us than he who is in the world. I feel like my moment of praise in this time was, letting God give me ways to overcome the feeling of loneliness by choosing to think creatively or out of the box about my situation. Maybe we are all practicing how we can creatively connect with others despite the pandemic with technology. Keep praising the Lord with joy, no matter what the circumstances you face!

Dear Jesus, God, thank You for the family of God. Jesus, You choose to be the hands and feet through Christians and touch our lives. God, You are love and have designed us to live in community. God, I need others, and I need You, thank You that it's Your design for us. You are the One who provides the right people in my life. I will keep praising You and thanking

You for the life that You give me. You are holding my life in the palm of Your hands. Amen

Tanja first started writing as a songwriter, as she had a passion for singing and worship ministry. Writing continued to be a part of her journey through creative writing, personal journaling, and later blogging. When Tanja became a teacher, she became more interested in studying the Bible, which led her to the United States as a Bible student. When she returned to Australia and continued teaching, she also studied a Master of Arts in Biblical Studies. Tanja is trilingual and has lived in Australia, Japan, and the United States.

She desires to lead her reader to know Christ more, for people to find their identity and healing in Christ. She is a continuous student of the Word of God and loves to share what God has done in her life. She currently lives in Brisbane, Australia.

You can find more of her work at www.tanjawrites.com

TEN

Beloved

TANJA TUOVINEN

"And when Jesus was baptized, immediately he went up from the water, and behold, the heavens were opened to him, and he saw the Spirit of God descending like a dove and coming to rest on him; and behold, a voice from heaven said, "This is my beloved Son, with whom I am well pleased." — Mark 3:16-17

When I was writing a theology thesis paper for my Master of Arts degree, Easter morning arrived, and I drove my dad to an Easter service. My dad was leading the meeting. I had come from the highway onto a slip-road that turned to the left. I was waiting for some cars to drive by when a heavy vehicle behind me slammed into the back of my car. The damage wasn't severe, and the driver who had hit my car was from another Australian state and apologized for the inconvenience. I was able to continue driving, and before I went to the meeting, I rang my insurance company. After the session had ended, my friend greeted me and had coffee with me. She had heard of what had happened and was sympathetic. After coffee, we went to another Easter meeting at a different location. At that worship service, I remember pouring my heart into the worship that day and singing with tears rolling down my face.

Sometime later, I met my mentor, where I talked about my progress with my studies and research. I told her I had felt like the enemy hated what I was doing, and it seemed like he was after me. She looked at me and said, "Do you know that you are the daughter of the King?" It was so simple, yet it suddenly occurred to me that for a while, I had forgotten that I was the daughter of the King. Why had I forgotten such an important yet simple truth of being a Christian?

When I was younger, that was what I had believed. I had so many adventures with God because I had understood who I was in Christ. That is all it took, "believe that you are the daughter of the King," that was key!

That day I had to relearn that I was the daughter of the King. I am God's beloved, and I am a new creation because of Jesus. I can call to God as my Abba, Father because I am His daughter.

In the wilderness, don't forget who you are, if you have good things happening, don't forget who you are. Don't forget if all is being taken from you or you feel like you're being tested.

That was key for Jesus, when He was in the wilderness, He didn't forget who He was. The devil tried to tempt Him to get His glory right away if He only bowed down to Satan. Jesus never bowed down to the devil. Jesus had a significant purpose to fulfill that affected you and me. He claimed victory over sin and death when He died on Calvary. Jesus knew, and He believed that He was the beloved Son of God. After Jesus left His forty days in the desert, He got baptized, and Father God called out from heaven, "This is My Beloved Son!"

Don't forget that you are the daughter or son of God, and because of that, you have authority over the enemy, you too have a plan and purpose in the kingdom of God.

Dear Jesus, I worship You and adore You. Thank You for being an example for my life, I will follow You and be Your disciple. Lead me, guide me, and speak to me through the Holy Spirit. Show me the way in the wilderness, and let me give thanks to You for all You've done and will do in my life. Give me a song to sing when I am in the wilderness that will glorify Your name. Amen

ELEVEN

The Truth is You are His Treasure

TANJA TUOVINEN

"But you are a chosen people, a royal priesthood, a holy nation, God's special possession, that you may declare the praises of Him who called you out of darkness into His wonderful light." —1 Peter 2:9

"You are God's treasure!" Those were the last words I heard when I departed 'School of Worship' in Texas, USA. I had wanted to do this school in a mission's setting years before, but God opened the door for me to be there when it was even more meaningful and special to me. It was after a difficult season in my life, in that season, I had been hurt in the area concerning worship ministry. As a result of that season I faced a deep spiritual valley where even the simple thing of connecting with God in my quiet time was difficult, and I didn't want to hear music or worship songs. I felt rejection from leadership, which made me think God rejected me, and I felt like God didn't want me to worship Him. God not wanting you to worship Him is never the truth no matter who you are!

It was surprising that I should do the School of Worship, and it brought healing to me as a person. The course was a place where I felt I could use my giftings again with writing songs. I heard the truth about God's character with teaching. I went to Guatemala as outreach and recorded new songs with other worshippers.

As I have been writing this devotional, I have realised that the truth that I should have known all along is that I am God's treasure, and the greater purpose in being a worshipper of God is because we are His treasure that's why we should worship God. As Christians, we are His prize and are valuable to Him, He desires worship from us, and He has made a way for us to worship Him by rescuing us from sin.

God took the children of Israel out of Egypt and brought them through the desert into the Promised Land to worship Him, while doing so, He said to them, "you are my treasured possession."

Christians are God's treasured possession and have a purpose to worship God. He is a God who cares about the intimate details about you and knows your name. There are days when you might forget how precious you are to God, and you might let your feelings overwhelm you and believe in lies. The truth is that God calls you, His jewel! He wants to draw you nearer and closer to His heart. He desires that you will worship Him. Because of Jesus Christ, God sees righteousness in you and holiness. You are set apart, and He has called you to serve Him and worship Him. We can proclaim to the world that there is hope in the name of Jesus Christ.

Worship Jesus today and start lifting a new song to the King of Heaven.

> *Lord, I feel wounded, and I don't really know why. Bad circumstances have left me dry, and I'm meandering in this desert. It's hot, and I don't have water for my soul. My joy, my love, my energy, my hope, my desires, and my dreams have been shattered. Who should I turn to? Where should I look? My hope comes from You, no matter where I look, it comes from You, right? Please see me here, heal me and take me in your care. Amen*

TWELVE

Be Still

TANJA TUOVINEN

"He says, "Be still, and know that I am God; I will be exalted among the nations, I will be exalted in the earth." —Psalms 46:10

In my twenties, I saw the end of a romantic relationship while I was living in Japan. I was in Japan teaching English and doing music ministry at the time. However, the young man I was dating was living overseas. He didn't want to break up over the phone but broke up by email. The morning I read the email, I was devastated, despite that, I still went to work in my English teaching job.

I was living with my missionary parents in a Japanese apartment on the outskirts of Tokyo. That night when I came home, my mum had come from a women's meeting. I came in and hugged my mum and started crying for two or three minutes. My mum said, "What's wrong?" I just kept on crying. It was too painful to say it. I finally got the courage to blurt it out that my relationship had ended. My mum asked, "why?" It was just one of those moments where I couldn't really remember the reason but knew precisely what had happened. It was over!

After my mother and I talked for a while, my mum reasoned that "well, maybe he wasn't the one!" I agreed and remembered that he didn't even like the song "Amazing Grace." That was ironic since that was a song that I had sung at a church service, and he had complimented my singing voice.

A few days passed, and the breakup might have kept me down for weeks, months or even years. However, my mum had a word of the Lord for me. She said that she felt like the Lord was telling me to be still and know that God is God. That scripture verse Psalms 46:10 comforted me, and it made me hope that I had a future, and I didn't feel hopeless for very long. God picked me up and helped me see the future that I would be walking into with Him.

In that season, there was also worship songs that I held on to, like "Hear Our Praises," a Reuben Morgan song. I also would write my own songs.

Is Psalms 46 a Psalm that is important to you? Have you been through something in your life that God has pointed this Scripture out to you and said, just be still remember that I am God? What does it mean to be still?

The Hebrew word for 'still' is *raphah*, which is a verb that means; "to relax," "to cease," "to let drop," "to leave alone." One commentator says that it is like the verse is giving a command that says, "let go and let God do the work." We have to remind ourselves to let God do the fighting and the consulting. God fights for us! The more we pray, praise God and study about Him the more God's character will become clear, and we will know that we are in good hands.

In the ministry of Jesus (Mark 4:35-40), there was a day when He was teaching people about the kingdom of God. After His ministry time, he told his disciples that he wanted to cross the lake of Galilee. While he was sleeping, a fierce storm arose that frightened the disciples. The disciples panicked and said, "Jesus help us, we will die!" Jesus stilled the storm, that was a miracle! When you feel like you are drowning in your storms of life, know that God has the power to bring quiet. God is in control, and God is sovereign. We can be in awe of Him and His majesty. When you go through the storms of life, get your musical instruments, get a pen and paper, and write new songs of worship to the Lord. Remember His character, that He is faithful, He is merciful, He is kind, He is righteous and Holy, and He is loving.

Dear Jesus, a storm has come into my life right now, and it feels as strong as a Tsunami. The waves will crush me for sure, won't they? Will You come when I can't see You? Will You still the storms ranging before me? Are You in control when I feel chaos? God come and calm the storm. Let me worship You in a greater way and teach me who You are. Amen

THIRTEEN

Amazing Love

BECKY SIMS

"I will rejoice and be glad in Your faithful love because You have seen my affliction. You have known the troubles of my life and have not handed me over to the enemy. You have set my feet in a spacious place." —Psalm 31:7-8 (HCSB)

God of love and beauty divine.

Your lifeline is open no matter the time.

You know our thoughts and feelings, and provide for our healings. You save all the tears that we'll ever cry.

Your love, oh Lord, we cannot comprehend.

You promise to be with us in eternity with no end. In sickness or health, whether poor or with wealth, You have promised to stay close by us and help.

Thank You, Lord, for all that you do!

We long to share the love we've been given by You.

We pray to be helpful to those You send our way.

Allow us to be Your eyes, hands, and feet each day.

There's no way we can repay You for all You have done, for You sent us Your One and Only Son.

Through His life, death, and resurrection, our best is yet to come!

For when this life is over, You'll welcome us into Your heavenly home.

God's love is amazing! As Paul declares in Romans 8:38-39 (HCSB):

> "For I am persuaded that not even death or life, angels or rulers, things present or things to come, hostile powers, height or depth, or any other created thing will have the power to separate us from the love of God that is in Christ Jesus our Lord!"

> *Dear Lord, thank You for Your amazing love! You have given us so much! Help us to stay connected to You. Give us opportunities to share Your love each day. In Christ's name, Amen.*

> *Where do you see God's amazing love present in your life today?*

Becky Sims has a strong faith in Jesus and a love for writing encouraging letters to friends and others. She prays that her devotional blog and books will help other women longing to grow closer to the Lord to gain hope

and meaning in their lives, while looking forward with confidence to eternity in Heaven.

Becky is a wife and mother, Hope*Writer, former teacher, and author. She has been active in her church choir. She especially enjoys quiet time with the Lord and often spends time in her porch chair in prayer (click on the image or here).

https://beckysims.org/

FOURTEEN

Quiet Worship

BECKY SIMS

"Be still, and know that I am God. I will be exalted among the nations, I will be exalted in the earth!" — Psalm 46:10 (ESV)

At times, worship doesn't look like singing and praising the Lord for others to hear. When the world seems heavy and we are struggling to get through each moment, we don't have the energy to worship in big ways.

God doesn't ask us to be something that we're not. He honors our emotions and knows how we're feeling much deeper than we do. He loves us more than any human ever could. He longs to spend time with us, no matter what we are going through.

We can simply rest and be with Him. Breathe deeply. Whisper the Bible promises that are etched in your heart. Thank Him for another day; for His protection, guidance, love, faithfulness, and powerful presence in your life.

Notice the gifts He has given you. Thank Him for each one; the sunshine or rain, clean air, the scent and beauty of the wildflowers. Thank Him for your family members and friends.

Listen to some instrumental hymns or other soothing music. Hum along.

If you need even more rest and quiet, thank the Lord for the gift of sleep. Find a quiet place to take a nap. Say a prayer asking Him to handle all of your concerns for this time. He will lovingly accept.

You will find joy again. You'll return to singing and praising aloud. This quiet time you are spending with the Lord now will draw you closer to Him. Even Jesus needed to spend time on His own to pray, rest, and commune with His Father.

Dear Lord, thank You for the gift of quiet worship. We are thankful that You have created us with the ability to rest, reflect, and spend time with You. In Christ's name, Amen.

How will you spend time with the Lord this week? Where could you add some quiet worship?

FIFTEEN

Making Music

BECKY SIMS

"Come, let us shout joyfully to the Lord, shout triumphantly to the rock of our salvation! Let us enter His presence with thanksgiving; let us shout triumphantly to Him in song." —Psalm 95:1-2 (HCSB)

Music has always been important in my life. Singing along with Debby Boone songs in my mirror with my microphone was a high point of my free time growing up.

I even met my husband in the University Chorus.

Our house is full of music makers. My husband and sons play the drums. My older son also plays marimba and piano, while my younger son plays the piano and cello. I still love to sing!

We use our gifts at church on occasion and enjoy making joyful noises at home as well. It's a way to take a break and leave some of the stress behind by refocusing our minds.

Music enhances our worship. We can begin singing or playing songs to bring us back to the Lord.

We can also meditate on the words of hymns and other Christian music to help us in our worship time with the Lord. It allows us to be more open and connected to the Spirit.

At times, we may not feel much like worshiping through music. But I have found that when I start singing a hymn or other song with God's positive message, I find my mood lifting and my spirit becoming lighter.

Music is a creative outlet. Whether you enjoy making music, or listening to the music of others, it can help bring us closer to the Lord.

Dear Lord, thank You for the gift of music. Thank You for those who share their creative talents. Help remind us to sing joyfully to You! You alone are worthy of our praise! In Christ's name, Amen.

Which songs bring you closer to the Lord? How can you add more music into your week?

SIXTEEN

Prayer Walks

BECKY SIMS

"First of all, then, I urge that petitions, prayers, intercessions, and thanksgivings be made for everyone, for kings and all those who are in authority, so that we may lead a tranquil and quiet life in all godliness and dignity." —1 Timothy 2:1-2 (HCSB)

I enjoy walking and talking with the Lord. The time we spend together can help clear my mind and focus my thoughts. Prayer walks are a wonderful way to worship and connect with the Lord. They provide us with time to exercise our bodies while communing with God about what is on our minds and hearts.

When we are out in our neighborhoods, we can say "hi" to those who pass by. We can pray for the young mother pushing her child in the stroller, and those playing basketball at the local school playground. Let us express gratitude for those who serve us in the local stores or deliver our mail. We can ask for a positive welcome for those who recently moved in down the street.

We can pray for the traffic directors holding up the signs and those doing construction nearby.

The rhythmical movement of walking helps our prayers to flow. Looking around the environment, it is easy to see those who surround us. Some we know and interact with on occasion. Others we only see from a distance. We can still have a spiritual connection with them through the power of prayer.

Many times, we receive prayer requests from friends on social media and through others at church and work. This extended prayer time is the perfect time to talk with God about these concerns. He'll take our big issues and our simple daily questions and decisions, too. He is a great listener and rarely interrupts. But when He does, it is with a quiet presence that reassures and guides our path.

We can also ask for our needs. Carrying life's burdens alone is too much. Sharing these things with God provides us with power and strength.

Dear Lord, thank You for being with us no matter what we are doing. Thank you for the communities You have provided for us. Please help us to share our concerns with you. In Christ's name, Amen.

Write a list of current prayer requests. Come back and update your list often.

SEVENTEEN

Becoming a Worshiper

AMI LOPER

"But the hour is coming, and is now here, when the true worshipers will worship the Father in spirit and truth, for the Father is seeking such people to worship him." —John 4:23

The way that I perceive love is through verbal affirmations. Nothing makes me feel love quite like my husband telling me that he loves and appreciates me. However, his verbal affirmations of love take on a whole new dimension when he expresses that he loves me just for being me, when there is no other feeling expressed than pure adoration. "I love you" is wonderful (but a bit general) and "Thank you for my clean laundry" is great (but more about what I do than who I am), but "You are precious to me" does something altogether different in my heart.

I had a realization a few weeks ago. I love God more than I can express. I long to be nearer and nearer to Him. I long to know Him truly and intimately. At my core, I am a worshipper. But I've realized that so often when I speak my adoration to Him, it is either too rote or too much about me. Like those words of affirmation from my husband that are nice, I can say "I love you" forever and never reach the heart of worship. I can say, "God, thank You for what You've done for me" and never focus on just Him.

Like the Shulamite woman in the Song of Solomon, I can spark and rekindle my love and passion for the Lord by meditating on who He is. In chapter 5:10-16, the Beloved goes into great detail to recount the splendors of her Lover, describing Him with love and adoration.

In this section she is not recounting what He does that makes Him worthy of her love, she is simply praising who He is.

Surely, our Abba loves to be worshipped for all His wonderful deeds, for His loving kindness, for His saving hand, but consider also worshipping Him for His innate qualities.

What if we spent more time proclaiming our love and adoration for our Lord? When I turn my focus solely to exalting Him—not for what He's done (although, of course, there's ample place for that), but just for who He is, something amazing happens in my worship: My Lover shows up.

Something also happens in me: the needs I have are needs I know He will meet as I look into His eyes and see the Love that causes all worries to fade.

Jesus told the woman at the well in John 4:23-24 that the Father is seeking worshippers. Note that He is not seeking worship; He is seeking individuals who are worshippers. He seeks intimate relationship, not mental ascent. He desires people, not accolades.

Is our worship a reflection of that type of relationship? Is our worship calling out as "deep calls to deep," the worshipper calling out to the only Worthy One?

Lord, I want to do more than worship; I want to be a worshipper. Awaken the desire in me to be a true lover of Yours. Enlighten my eyes to see Your glory that I may worship You in the splendor of Your holiness. I thank You for all You've done and will do, but, Lord, I adore who You are!

Ami has been preaching since her teens and has her Master's Degree in Theology. A gleeful puzzler, a persistent solution-finder, a hunter of clarity, Ami finds her joy in discovering connections and truths tucked in corners of the Word of God.

As an author and a guest speaker in churches and conferences, she brings those truths to light as she crafts words that bring transformation. Ami's mission is to use the challenges she's been through to resource others into their freedom by bringing hope to the wounded, spiritual food to the hungry, tools to the learning, and kinship for the invisible.

Ami and her husband live in Arizona and love few things more than surrounding themselves with their children and their growing number of grandchildren.

Connect with Ami on her website, amiloper.com, and on the socials, where you can find her by name.

EIGHTEEN

Face to Face

AMI LOPER

"O my dove, in the clefts of the rock, in the crannies of the cliff, let me see your face, let me hear your voice, for your voice is sweet, and your face is lovely."
—Song of Solomon 2:14

Honestly, I was just trying to keep up as I dodged clumped groups of families and dashed after the little dark blonde curls that changed direction at random. Simultaneously, Little Miss Distractable's older brother was kicking up dirt and asking something about an ice cream cone. Their mom, my daughter, was slowly following behind with the toddling one-and-a-half-year-old littlest.

Elephants trumpeted and some wild bird's, "Cacaw!" floated over all the chatter. Agreement was finally made on the next exhibit to view and we made our way to the orangutan habitat like drunk butterflies amid too many flowers.

With her face against the Plexiglas, a small female orangutan sat perfectly still, staring out at everyone who was staring in. At first the kids went right past her; something so still rarely was noticed. But I called my three-and-a-half-year-old tousled granddaughter back so she could see this beautiful beast up close. She came right up to the glass (conveniently the same height as the sitting orangutan) and without hesitation she pressed her face against the glass. She stood there, herself now unusually still and quiet, her eyes locked with the ape's for a full minute before skipping away.

Weeks later I was in a worship service, and although I was worshiping, that image of my granddaughter and the orangutan kept coming back to my mind. As is my custom when random thoughts won't leave me alone, I asked the Lord why.

He brought another image to mind that gave me a clue as to what He was trying to get across to me. The image was the sign for "presence" from American Sign Language, which was my second language in college. In this sign, the hands are before the face, palms inward, facing one another, symbolizing two faces gazing at one another.

Instantly I knew what the Lord was trying to convey.

Time in the Secret Place. Time to be in His Presence, two faces meeting, locking eyes, gazing into one another, knitting our hearts together. Our Abba desires intimate times with each of us. He desires more than being sung *about*; He desires to be sung *to*. We are the unique creations that He fashioned for this Secret Place relationship.

There is no experience like letting the world, with its troubles and to-do's, fade into oblivion as nothing becomes more real to you than your Abba's face. There is nothing so freeing as the laying down of every burden, every care and letting the God of the universe sweep you off your feet.

It isn't about eloquence or loquaciousness; it is solely about connecting. Until you have connected, you haven't worshipped.

When I meet with my Lord in the Secret Place, this is my one goal and desire: to forget what weighs on my flesh, what weighs on my mind and commune with Him, face to face until eyes meet eyes, spirits connect and hearts meld into one.

> *Lord, I long for You, to be in that place where I look into Your eyes, where I feel Your heart, where I am connected to You. I know Your desire is for me to meet with You, too. Help me, Lord, as I draw near to not just go through the motions of spending a set amount of time or saying a set of words, but help me to actually connect with You.*

NINETEEN

God's Desire vs. Mine

AMI LOPER

"For as high as the heavens are above the earth, so great is his steadfast love toward those who fear him."
—Psalms 103:11

Music fades from my ears and words cease their flow from my lips as I am suddenly fully alert and aware of something that I was oblivious to the moment before. My body may be standing in church, but I am simultaneously in another place altogether. I am standing before the Lord. I feel His Presence and faith hangs on to the truth that God is here with me.

There are moments I am so caught up in prayer or worship that the whole world fades away and I see and feel nothing but God. It is glorious and my constantly flitting mind tries to stay there as long as possible. I can feel my desire so intensely and be calling out for Him... yet, moments later, be contemplating a completely random thought.

God's desire is so much deeper than mine. His desire is more faithful, more constant. I go through times in my life that I am so on fire, in love with God that I feel I could spontaneously combust! But there are also seasons of laziness or busyness. God's desire is unfading, and He desires me when I desire Him with intensity though He knows my intensity will wane. He is always waiting and desiring our devotion.

In spite of me, He loves me. He desires me when I am at my worst. He desires me when I am angry with Him. He desires me when I am cold and uncaring. He desires me regardless of my past, present and future sins. He is perfect in His desire.

The desire to connect with the human race has been God's desire throughout time. He is in search of a lover, one who will give oneself to Him completely. One who cares to know His heart and who will adopt it as their own. The desire we feel for Him, no matter how strong we feel it, is merely a taste of the desire God feels toward us.

Any "good" human emotion we have, God has and in its perfect form. Since every good and perfect gift comes from the Lord and God gives good things out of His abundance, we can surmise that "good" desires are not only His creation, but that they also originate in Him. They are His desires to begin with. If we desire intimacy with Him, should we not, by the very existence of that godly desire, know that He also has that desire toward us? And if God has a desire, should we not also know that His is the purest, most perfect, constant expression of that desire?

We could never love God more than He loves us. We could never desire Him more than He desires us. Our passion for Him is a mere glimpse of His great passion for us. And we can trust the heart of God toward us, knowing that our fulfillment in Him is His primary goal.

> *Lord, if I'm honest, sometimes I feel overwhelming joy and adoration in Your Presence and other times, I can hardly get my brain to focus. Lord, I am so grateful that Your ways are so much higher than mine. I'm so glad that even in my best moments of attentiveness and love, my best is only a dim reflection of Your great desire for me. That overwhelms my heart, Abba. Thank You for loving me like that.*

TWENTY

Veilless Worship

AMI LOPER

"Therefore, brothers, since we have confidence to enter the holy places by the blood of Jesus, by the new and living way that he opened for us through the curtain, that is, through his flesh..., let us draw near..." Hebrews 10:19-20, 22

It felt like a wet, icy blanket had been wrapped around my shoulders. In this place where love and warmth should be the abiding sense, I felt distant ambivalence. I felt lonelier in that moment with loved ones than if I had been in the least inhabited place on earth.

Have you ever been in a relationship in which you felt more solitary in the relationship than without? You can hardly call that relationship at all.

Under the Old Covenant (in the Old Testament), few people pressed past the mandated distance that people had chosen to erect between man and God. In Exodus 19, we read of their choice of comfortable distance and

God's acceptance of their weak faith that required mediators and veils to shield them from His glory.

Not David though.

It seems some are such people after the heart of God that they can pull the heartstrings of God and cause Him to give freely what might otherwise be held in reserve for a later time. Mary, the mother of Jesus, did this. And Jesus responded, "My hour has not yet come," but then promptly did what Mary asked (John 2:4).

David pulled on God's heart and timing too.

David was a prophet of sorts (Acts 2:29-30). David not only spoke prophetically, he also lived prophetically. He reached into what would only be permitted in the New Covenant and he dragged it into the Old Covenant. The type of relationship he reached with God was largely unknown in the Old Covenant. Only a few people obtained it. It was a relationship in which the veil was torn away between the worshipper and God.

David brought the Ark of the Covenant into Jerusalem long years after it had been captured by the Philistines. When he brought it into the city, he worshipped before it and placed it in a tent adjacent to his own residence. He offered sacrifices before the Ark, but after the initial animal sacrifices, the only sacrifice at the Ark for the many years until Solomon built the Temple, was worship (1 Chron. 16:4-7, 37-38).

Only in the New Covenant would such worship be fully restored to humankind—worship that was face to face, veilless adoration of God. With the Temple's rent veil at the death of Jesus, the tent of David was restored

(Amos 9:11). Intimacy with God was opened to all who would come through the broken veil, Jesus (Heb. 10:20).

The heart of God has never ceased to long for the intimate relationship we were created to have. He has never stopped in His pursuit. The only thing that has stopped Him is the limitations set by the people He is pursuing, for He will not force His love and affection where it is not wanted. Those who have welcomed His love, have received it in abundance. Those who have settled for an arm's length distance between themselves and the Great God of the Universe have received just what they wanted. Yet, God has never stopped yearning nor communicating His desire to His people.

> *Lord, I'm no longer content with comfortable distance between us. I want more of You in my life, Lord. And although I know it will require my effort, my devotion, my time, I am willing to give all to have more of You. My heart aches for You. I trust that as I draw near to You, You will draw near to me.*

TWENTY-ONE

Worship in the Waiting Room

TANYA DUFFEY

"Do not be anxious about anything, but in every situation, by prayer and petition, with thanksgiving, present your requests to God. And the peace of God, which transcends all understanding, will guard your hearts and your minds in Christ Jesus." —Philippians 4:6-7

I've spent my fair share of times in this life waiting. I'm certain you have too. But what about the seasons of life when we are praying desperately for God to intervene in a specific situation yet day after day, night after night, we wake up to see the situation is the same? That's where I found myself for the entire year of 2019. That year my dad had faced multiple health issues and it seemed they grew more complicated by the day. He spent more time in the ICU of our local hospital that year than he did at my parent's home. That meant most of my days, and many nights were spent in the waiting room. It was a space I can still vividly see. The stark walls, hard floors, and stiff chairs. Sometimes we would share the space with another family waiting on news of their loved one and sometimes we sat alone, in silence mostly. I remember specifically one morning as the sun was coming up and shining through the windows of the room. Being in the ICU, we couldn't stay in the room with my dad but they allowed us to stay in the waiting area. I decided to go ahead and get up from the makeshift "bed" my mom and I had pulled together with chairs and a couple of blankets. As I sat there, pulling up my morning devotion to read and have prayer before the day of more waiting began, I felt the slightest tug on my heart. It was as if the Holy Spirit was saying, "I am here with you. I hear your prayers." It's so difficult to describe in words what this did to my spirit that day. But that morning my desperate prayers for my dad's health switched to worship and praising my Savior in that waiting room. I realized he was hearing our pleas and he was in fact with my dad and with us as a family in our darkest hour. I began changing my questions of why is this happening to, "Lord, I give this to you and I will honor and praise you in this waiting room. I will worship you in this storm!"

As time went on during that year of waiting in the literal tiny waiting room of the hospital and in waiting on God, my faith grew, and others witnessed Christ. No, it was not and would never be my desire for my dad and our family to have walked through so much that year but in that time, God was glorified, and for that, I am forever grateful. During this time, nurses would walk into the room and say they felt Jesus near. Doctors made comments about dad being a miracle and feeling

God's presence. The day my dad was to be discharged for the last time there was one specific nurse who even sought us out in the waiting room. She shared that witnessing our faith in Christ rekindled and strengthened her faith in him again. So many blessings came from the darkest and scariest time. And I learned a valuable lesson... To worship God in the waiting rooms of life.

Friend, I don't know what heavy burden you are walking through today. But I do know God knows and oh how he cares so deeply for you. He longs to walk with you and hold you up today. When we choose to worship in our waiting we gain perspective for the bigger picture, wisdom, our faith is strengthened, and our testimony shines a light for others to gain hope and strength from. As we unclench the tight grip on our circumstances, and with our hands open and lifted to our Lord, saying "I trust you Lord and I worship you while I wait", we will see his hand in our lives.

He sees you.

He hears you.

He is with you.

> *Lord, we don't like this waiting part of life. Sometimes it hurts so much we feel we can't handle another day. Please help us take our eyes off of our circumstances and shift them toward you. Your love for us is all-encompassing. You are a good good Father and we can trust you. We worship you while waiting on you, Lord. Amen.*

http://thejourney-home.com/

TWENTY-TWO

My Heart of Worship

IRISH GAMBITO

"Though the fig tree may not blossom, Nor fruit be on the vines; Though the labour of the olive may fail, And the fields yield no food; Though the flock may be cut off from the fold, And there be no herd in the stalls—Yet I will rejoice in the LORD, I will joy in the God of my salvation." —Habakkuk 3:17-18 (NKJV)

Where is my worship coming from?

Worship is giving reverence to a divine being. The Bible says in 1 Corinthians 10:31, whatever we do, do all to the glory of God. Whether you speak, think, eat, play, work, whatever it is, we must do it in reverence to the Lord. Before the Lord opened my heart to understand the heart of Jesus, I was carelessly doing things without the mindset of making it to worship. I thought worshipping Him was merely on the service of attending church, singing praises to Him, being involved in church ministries. Thus, I did not grasp the real meaning of worship in my daily walk with Jesus. But I separated worship from service of ministering in the church rather than making it a habit in my everyday walk with Jesus.

When the Lord broke the silence of my reality with my Christian walk, it drew me to see beyond what was inside of me. It was at the breaking point in my life through the betrayal of my marriage, as adultery, that the Lord revealed the true condition of my heart. And everything in me was falling apart emotionally. The hurt and anger I had was too much to bear. There were times, I had my unguarded moment with my angry heart and led me to sin. I lived daily with anger, hurt, and threw myself into the self-pity party.

I thought for such a long time that I was serving the Lord with all my heart and strength. But God showed me I had a self-serving heart. Apparently, my emotions controlled me over the things what was happening in my marriage. I should have gracefully loved and forgave him. That being said, I merely served my feelings and thoughts- that's not worship to God. It turned out I shove him into reading the Bible, pray, and see him as the spiritual leader in the family. In other words, I was trying to change him. And the worries of not changing him consumed me.

It came to my turning point that the Lord confronted me with my anger through my bible reading that led to Ezekiel 36:26-27. God can turn our stony heart into a heart of flesh, as gentle and forgiving. That's when I turned my heart of worship to Him instead of myself. Sometimes we forget to worship the Lord and we just lay hold of our good desires. We create our worship for ourselves instead of for the Lord. So, when betrayal hits my marriage, I was so devastated. That my heart was not ready to break the worship I had for myself, instead of the place for God's glory. The plans and goals I had for my family were solely to serve me, not the Lord. When we are in the wilderness of brokenness, it reveals the priority of our worship.

Do we worship ourselves or God? What is my heart's condition before the Lord? Does my good desire for others serve me or God?

Almighty Heavenly Father, I adore Your glory and wonders. You are a faithful Father. I worship You in Spirit and truth. Thank you for Your unending compassion and love when I feel worthless. Forgive me if I misjudged others because of my selfish motive. Lead me to receive Your forgiveness and deliverance. Help me live through the lens of your eyes and heart. Empower me with the Holy Spirit to unleash the worship I have for you. In Jesus' Name. Amen.

Find more from Irish Gambito on Amazon and at
www.betoughyetgentleinspirit.com

TWENTY-THREE

Hearts Can Change

SHARON HAZEL

"The LORD is my strength and song, and He has become my salvation; He is my God, and I will praise Him." —Exodus 15:2 (NKJV)

I love this verse of Scripture for the way it declares that the Lord *is* our strength and song. It doesn't say that He was, or that He might be, but boldly declares that He *is*! It became a verse that I clung to through a difficult period of my life. It was a time when my husband was struggling with long-term sickness, which brought uncertainty and fear for the future - everything that we thought was important seemed to be under threat. But the confident assurance of these words was a comfort, and a challenge.

This verse is part of the celebration song by Moses and Miriam after God had made the way for the Israelites to cross safely through the Red Sea. They had escaped from the danger of Pharaoh's pursuing army, finally they had left Egypt and captivity behind. In fact, they had left with blessing, with clothing, silver, and gold, and ahead for the first time in their lives was freedom. They were going on a three-day journey to worship at the Mountain of God!

These words are part of a spontaneous victory song, delighting in God's deliverance. Worshipping God is the natural response of thankful and grateful hearts. But sometimes the challenge is to declare this verse of praise and worship to God in and through the difficult times - those seasons when life seems to be a real struggle.

I had never been a music lover or a singer, but through a 'wilderness' season I learnt to sing. Not always very tunefully, even a little off key, but always from the heart. It is powerful when we engage with worshipping God in song – our praise and worship lifts our thoughts off ourselves and onto God.

When our focus becomes our Heavenly Father, there is a shift and a change in our perspective. Suddenly, in the light of God's love for us, our problems start to diminish, and hope begins to stir! As we praise God, we become more aware of His presence and remember that Jesus *is* our salvation. He *has* made the way to reconcile us to the Father. God is not remote and distant but is personal and intentional towards us, working for our good!

Praise and worship are not always spontaneous, sometimes it takes a conscious effort to say we *will* praise Him. We are choosing to praise God, through our difficulties and uncertainties, because He is faithful. He is more than able to bring us out of that season with blessing, stronger than when we went in. It is through trusting in the goodness of God that our faith grows, and it is in our song, the praise and worship of our heart, that we find strength.

"Do not sorrow, for the joy of the Lord is your strength." —Nehemiah 8:10 (NKJV)

Lord Jesus, I choose to praise You from a thankful and grateful heart because You are my salvation, You are my strength, and You are my song. Lord, I reflect on the wonder of Your unfailing love, that You never let me go, that You are with me every moment of the day, and You are worthy of all my worship. Amen.

https://limitless-horizon.com

TWENTY-FOUR

Worship Like Job

LAUREN ROSKILLY

> Then Job arose and tore his robe and shaved his head and fell on the ground and worshiped. And he said, "Naked I came from my mother's womb, and naked shall I return. The Lord gave, and the Lord has taken away; blessed be the name of the Lord." —Job 1:20-21

Job is a man who went through all kinds of trouble and trials, he had his family, livelihood and much more taken away from him. He was, what some may deem, "at rock bottom!" Imagine if you went through everything Job did.

How would that make you feel?

Angry? Depressed? Grief? Sad? Lonely? Anxious? Hurt? Rejected?

And I wouldn't blame you! When I went through some struggles in life (illness, poverty, homelessness etc) I was grieved to the point of depression.

Job felt most of the above too, well, he is human as well!

BUT

Here's the big *but*; despite all of this and how he felt about his situation, he still knew the Lord and who he was and is and he; Job, still fell to the ground and worshipped. Over the years, it wasn't an overnight thing by the way, through my faith and trust in God, I learned to build resilience. Remaining focused on Him, despite what was going on in my own situation.

So, we can take this scripture and remind ourselves, yes, we are human, but also, most importantly, we have the Lord, who does give and take away but is worthy to be praised, and at all times, even in those storms.

Life is full of ups and downs, so it is helpful to remember that trials and problems are to be expected. We are on a sinful earth, after all! But, the one thing in this world that is consistent, good, perfect, awesome is God, the Father, the creator and His son, Jesus, our saviour and He is worthy to be praised.

So, can I challenge you to find a worship song, or playlist, that resonates with you, to listen to next time you are feeling, what we might deem to be, negative emotions, or are going through particular trials or storms?

Dear Lord, thank you for this life. Thank you for your son who saved me. Thank you for the ups and the downs. Please help me to be grateful through all things. Please help me to worship through all things. Help me to understand I am human, but to know you are God; consistent, unchanging, faithful God. The God who gives and takes away. Thank you, Lord for everything. In Jesus' name, Amen

---

www.mindfulofchrist.net

TWENTY-FIVE

Should Worship Wear You Out?

NCR

"Even when I don't see it, You're working.

Even when I can't feel it, You're working.

You never stop, You never stop working."

—"Waymaker" song lyrics

I have been in many different churches and experienced many different worship sessions. Some churches, like the small 7th-day Adventist church that my grandmother attends, lack a worshipful experience. It usually consists of one or two hymns, and besides that, the church is filled with elderly people and grandpa-aged men who never liked to sing as boys and never learned to love to sing praise to God*. Other churches on the other hand have long drawn out two or three-hour worship experiences. I have (experienced or) witnessed a few of those times, as a bystander it almost seems like they are overdoing it. And when it comes to worship is easy to be just that, a bystander.

I currently work at Allaso Ranch and Retreat Center where a lot of interesting groups come. The different groups worship God in different ways. The group that is currently here—UPPERROOM young adults—has amazing several-hour worship experiences. One of my friends and co-workers said that she would get worn out if she worshiped God like that.

Should worship wear you out? Maybe that is the way some people like to worship God. But what about those who don't like to worship that way? My question for you is: "is it really worship if you are thinking about how you are not enjoying it?". And another thing that comes into play here is Satan trying to get us to think that we are not really worshiping God unless we are doing it a certain way. Don't let Satan shame you into thinking that worship is a chore you have to do as a good Christian and you have to do it in a certain way.

I don't know about you, but I don't want to just be a bystander. If we were having a one on one conversation together maybe we could discuss the different ways we worship God and the different ways to worship God, and which way works best for each of us individually. But since I am writing something on worship, I just want to encourage you to think as you read this.

"The chief end of man is to glorify God by enjoying him forever", that is one of my favorite quotes. God desires a real relationship with you. He also desires real worship. Worshiping God shouldn't wear you out. It shouldn't drain you of energy. It shouldn't be something you dread. It should be something you enjoy.

I could say much more about worship, but maybe I will let my fellow writers share some wisdom. I hope you to start enjoying God more as you make him the focus of your worship and thoughts.

*P.S. I hope I was clear enough that you don't have to sing or dance to worship. Yes, that is the way most people worship God. But that doesn't mean you have to worship God in that way. Above all let your worship for God be real and enjoyable.

Make this your prayer today:

"I'm coming back to the heart of worship

And it's all about You, it's all about You, Jesus

I'm sorry, Lord, for the thing I've made it

When it's all about You, it's all about You, Jesus"

—*"The Heart Of Worship" song lyrics by Matt Redman*

Find more from NCR on Amazon and the SunShining Podcast

TWENTY-SIX

The Eyes of the Lord See All

MIRANDA J. CHIVERS

"The eyes of the Lord are on the righteous, and his ears are attentive to their cry; but the face of the Lord is against those who do evil, to blot out their name from the earth." —Psalm 34:16

God hears us when we cry. What a blessed promise! He will reward the righteous and judge evil. More promises. The Bible encourages us to persevere and hold on to hope. We're challenged to focus on the Almighty's words and believe the timeless truth.

On a visit to Israel, we stopped at the Ein Gedi National Park, where David hid from King Saul. It's easy for an inexperienced hiker to get lost in this bleak, hilly desert wilderness. Guides provide safety from the sharp cliffs, deep caverns and treacherous trails. It's hard to believe anything except mountain goats can live here. But in the middle of this challenging terrain, there's a quiet oasis with tall acacia trees and a clear, cool stream. And the wildlife is plentiful.

God always provides.

Here, I could imagine David hiding in the cave when King Saul walked in for his private time. I could see how he stole through the darkness and sliced off a piece of Saul's robe. He could have killed him there, but David refused to silence God's chosen king. David was honorable and did the right thing.

How often do we find ourselves in similar circumstances? When life becomes unfair, we flee into the wilderness of suffering. We lick our wounds and seek revenge. "Our accusers must account for their wrongs," we scream. "Justice must be done."

We want to fight back, get even, or see them suffer. But instead, we pay the price while they get rewarded. And we wonder why God doesn't intervene.

Instead, God stays silent and watches. He sees all. He waits for us to choose our response to the injustice. In every trial, we have choices.

In my new series, *Russian Mennonite Chronicles (Book One: Katarina's Dark Shadow)* my characters Katarina and Anna must endure the Russian civil war, relying only on their wit and faith to get them through. Like David, they want God to intervene and rescue them. They're not expecting to hike along a mountainous path or find shelter in hidden caverns. The journey and destination are all unknown and the future looks very dark.

Throughout history, women have faced assaulting circumstances and been forced to protect their families under the most austere conditions. Like David, the characters in my books cry out to God for help, but they always choose to do the right thing and wait for God's justice. And they step onto the treacherous trail, believing God will hold their hand and keep them safe.

Real life doesn't guarantee happy endings on our timetable. But if we keep our eyes on Jesus, we are assured that He hears, He sees, and He will provide sustenance for the journey. The righteous live by faith. (Romans 1:17)

> *Dear Lord, please forgive me for doubting you. My situation seems unbearable and unfair. Help me trust that justice will be served and that my hard trials will be redeemed for your glory.*

Miranda J. Chivers is an award-winning Canadian Christian author. Writing historical fiction as MJ

Krause-Chivers, she's currently working on a suspense-filled series set during the Russian civil war in Ukraine.

Amazon.com/author/mirandajchivers

TWENTY-SEVEN

The Wilderness Journey

MIRANDA J. CHIVERS

"Before I formed you in the womb I knew you, before you were born I set you apart; I appointed you as a prophet to the nations." —Jeremiah 1:5 (NIV)

The negative circumstances of life have often caught me unprepared. Too often, I've taken the wrong road or stumbled over rocks along the way. Many uncontrollable events have veered me off course and stretched my faith. I've struggled with doubt.

I've persevered through the desert times while wondering if God really cared about me; and I've coped with almost unbearable loneliness during chronic illnesses, the death of loved ones, and the rejection by friends and family. Patience and resilience grew despite the uncertainty of forest times when I thought I'd never find my way out — like that unwanted divorce, times of financial crisis, the fear of losing my eyesight, and the frustration of living with a brain injury. And let's not forget those other valleys when I carried burdens that didn't belong to me and hiked down trails where I had no business. God never left me.

Staying the course has not been easy. But amid chaos, I've learned to trust God. And along the way, I've gained nuggets of wisdom. I'd like to share some with you.

- Life isn't easy. It's not meant to be. Keep in mind that Jesus didn't take the soft road to the cross. God assigned him the mission to save the world, but he could have quit at any point. Satan tempted him, friends betrayed him, one stole from him, the jealous attacked him, and public opinion railed against him. Money, friendship, and popularity couldn't persuade him to give up.
- We must stay the course and keep the goal in focus at all times. We'll reach the finish line by taking one step at a time. Like Jesus, if we want to get out of the wilderness, we must set our faces like flint and persevere.
- Whining about life doesn't accomplish or change anything. Jesus never complained about his assignment, although he begged God to take it away. Negative circumstances are inevitable, but it's how we handle those difficulties that label us as winners or losers. It's not whether we win or lose, but how we play the game that matters.
- All challenges are easier when you face them with a positive mindset. Be persistent in searching for the silver lining inside the dark cloud. Jesus didn't enjoy going to the cross. But

he focused on the bigger purpose behind the trial, even though it seemed impossible. The end will look better than the beginning.

- Jesus never lost sight of who he was. And neither should we. We are created in his image, designed by him, and admired and loved for who we are. All our mental or physical defects, personality traits and our eccentric ways are all part of our beauty. Our DNA is unique — like the snowflakes that fall from the sky — no two are the same. I may not like my thick thighs, my narrow eyes, or that scar above my lip, but God thinks I'm beautiful. And the master architect gave me special skills and attributes to fulfill the calling on my life, I must embrace my design.
- Never compare successes and failures. This is my road and my calling. I am no better or worse than another. God only asks me to do my best with the energy and skills he's given me. When I fall down, I simply need to stand up and try again.
- Forgive always. Never hold grudges.
- No matter what happens, God loves me and accepts me as I am.
- Thank God for the trials. Everything is for my good. I'm growing in wisdom, patience and perseverance.
- Pain increases my compassion for others and it teaches me to love more.

There is no valley, mountain, forest or desert where God cannot find us. Faith is a journey. The test is to trust the guide

Heavenly Father, thank you for reminding me that you have designed me for a purpose and are perfecting me for your glory. Help me keep my eyes on the road ahead and stop focusing on the pitfalls in the way. I trust you will bring me safely to the other side.

TWENTY-EIGHT

The Act of Worship

ERIN WATSON MOHR

"But the LORD said to Samuel, "Do not consider his appearance or his height, for I have rejected him. The LORD does not look at the things people look at. People look at the outward appearance, but the LORD looks at the heart." —1 Samuel 16:7

Worship is the greatest calling that we have upon our lives. It is a privilege to get to worship the God who created us, who knew us before we were born and took time with every detail and fibre of our being. Worship is a lifestyle.

I have been a worship leader for most of my life, been on many stages around the world and been involved with participating and leading various worship teams. If there is anything I would love to communicate about worship is that it is not a one day a week event. Worship is meant to be a twenty four hour around the clock lifestyle that frames how we participate in all the areas of our life.

Worship is not about perfectionism in musical skill and having the right line up for a service. (although being a musician, I cannot argue that being excellent at the craft is important). However, excellence is not to be confused with being perfect. Excellence is a heart posture and God is always more concerned about the inside of us than the appearances on the outside.

God gives us a powerful key regarding worship in this verse. It's literally like He is giving away His most valuable secrets and letting us in on what matters most to Him. I have learned that what the world deems as important versus what God considers important are very different things. Concerning the matter of worship it is critical to understand that the heart is the most desirable part of what God wants from us.

We can offer our perfect guitar solo, or that killer vocal line but if the heart is not engaged in the attitude of worship, it is rejected by the Lord. Scripture makes mention that while lips were uttering the proper protocol from particular people, hearts were far removed from what was actually being said. This is called lip service and it is an abomination to the Lord. It is the least authentic type of worship.

I have learned that God is always after the heart. It is the place He seeks after for intimacy with us. When we can lay aside our image, our thoughts of perfectionism and embrace the beauty of coming just as we are before the King of Kings, then we offer the truest and most valuable gift we have to give...our heart. This my friend is the purest act of worship, which is really all He has ever wanted from us. I encourage you to take off the mask of performance and let go of anything that hinders you from offering your heart.

Lord, creator of heaven and earth, I come before your throne just as I am. In the present space that I am in, I offer my heart to you as my sincere gift of worship. Help me to become more aware of the fact that all you really want is the real me, masks removed and unashamedly real. I choose to set myself free from any worldly standard of performance. It's not how well I can do something that moves your heart towards me, it's about me acknowledging my weaknesses and moving closer towards you so I can be wrapped in your strength. Thank you for leading me to the truth. I choose to fix my affections upon you and surrender my heart to the one who knows it better than anyone else. Eternally grateful, Amen.

Find Erin on Amazon and visit www.emergecoaching.ca

TWENTY-NINE

Rooted in Worship

KATIE ARTHUR

"Stand up and bless the Lord your God from everlasting to everlasting. Blessed be your glorious name, which is exalted above all blessing and praise."
—Nehemiah 9:5

My son was six years old when the COVID-19 Pandemic sent us home for months on end and the world shut down. With the gift of time handed to us, I wanted to be intentional in discipling him in his spiritual walk. I wanted something simple, but meaningful that would take my son's roots deeper and inform his spiritual walk throughout his life. This is when I discovered a beautiful new practice that Songwriters Keith and Kristyn Getty introduced to their daughters. Each month they focus on a new hymn and sing it every night before bed. These hymns are theologically rich with Biblical truth. It is these kinds of songs that, when sung back to the Lord, root us in worship.

Roots are an essential part of a living plant and without them, plants die. The plant's roots serve very specific purposes: providing stability, feeding the plant, and storing water and nutrients. When a plant has a well established root system, it is able to withstand strong storms, continue growing, and survive when drought strikes. Similarly, our relationship with God needs to have roots.

One such rooting that must take place in the life of a believer is that of worship. Worship is a practice of recognition of who God is through the attribution of reverence and honor. In worship, the truth of God's character and what he has done for us is acknowledged. As a result, our worship roots us, providing stability in our soil (God), feeding us (filling us with truth), and storing up water and nutrients (truths to remember when we struggle to see God working). With a good root system worship is both informed by and informs how we view God, ourselves, and others.

In the book of Nehemiah, when the city of Judah and people of Israel were restored, Nehemiah writes a prayer of worship, acknowledging all that God has done for His people. This act of worship is informed by Nehemiah's correct view of God, himself, and others. As a result this worship informs the people of Israel's view of God, themselves, and others, further rooting them in their relationship with God. Rooting yourself in the practice of worship as Nehemiah did is life changing for not only you, but those around you.

Lord, thank you for giving us timeless truth that we can hold fast to. As I grow in my spiritual walk, help me to root myself in these truths through worship of you. May my worship strengthen me to withstand the seasons of storm and drought that will come. As I root my life in worship, draw the hearts of those around me and shape my view of you, myself, and others. Amen.

Find out more about Katie at
https://themismatchedwife.com/

THIRTY

Simple Worship

ROBERT KAPEN

"Praise the Lord, my soul; all my inmost being, praise his holy name." —Psalms 103:1

Worship is the act of praising God. It doesn't mean just singing to, or about God once a week on Sundays. Yes, lifting hands, closing your eye's, and shouting praises to your Savior is amazing and wonderful. I love putting on my headphones, throwing on a worship song, and cranking up the volume. It's one way I get filled and renewed spiritually. If we are to follow the bible; and worship music is in there to be a helpful tool for us, we would be unwise not to participate. So, I am not saying it is a bad thing, but that isn't the only way we can praise and worship the Lord. By only worshipping the Lord through songs we limit His grandeur and essentially put God in a box, when His love, strength, and grace or so much bigger. There are other ways to bring Him praise that don't involve a song.

One way I have found, is in our actions or how people see us interact out in society. I love when people say, "there is something different about you" after doing something for Christ. I know in that moment I know I'm giving praise to God and at that time they can see him in my worshipping. I love when He gives me strength to do something I thought was impossible. But with Him in my corner I am able to accomplish it and in doing so I'm pointing towards Him, praising and worshipping His holy name. I know that it's worship when I do good things in His name, because I can feel God filling me with His spirit and other people reap the benefits of the fruit that is produced from it.

The second way I have found is a little similar but It's more personal. It is acts for yourself, your one on one alone time with the creator of the universe. For me before my illness that paralyzed me, my worship was in my hands. Now what do I mean by that, I loved working with my hands and being active. For example, washing my truck because it was a chunk of time where I wasn't bothered and I could pray, praise and reflect on God and His hand in my life. Also, riding my bike at night through town. It was mindless work but it put me in a place of praising, worshiping and pouring into God, while He poured back into me.

The last way I've experienced true worship is writing about Him. Then being able to see His goodness through your life. I witnessed it first hand when I had just gone through a life altering and traumatic experience. When it first happened, writing was a way to process everything. When I wrote about all His promises and the different truth's He lays out in the bible I get filled with His peace, comfort, strength, hope, and wisdom. Then while I'm writing it becomes almost a dance back and forth, as I praise Him and in return, He breathes the fruits of the spirit back into me. That's why I think it is a great idea to have a journal near by when you are alone reading the bible. Because while you are praising Him and reviewing His words, it gives Christ a wider window to pour into you, refresh you, give you things you might need, or just continue to allow you to center your focus on Him.

God, help me to worship by centering my focus on Christ, praising and pouring into You while You pour back into me with the fruits of Your spirit.

Discover more from Kapen on Amazon.

THIRTY-ONE

Days of Worship

LEENA J

"I appeal to you therefore, brothers, by the mercies of God, to present your bodies as a living sacrifice, holy and acceptable to God, which is your spiritual worship. Do not be conformed to this world, but be transformed by the renewal of your mind, that by testing you may discern what is the will of God, what is good and acceptable and perfect." —Romans 12: 1-2

A few years ago I read an interview with a popular actor who vulnerably stated that she wanted to make her life "an act of worship." I don't remember if it was originally a quote she had heard/read elsewhere, but I remember having to pause. Something about her statement reminded me of the first two verses in Romans 12. To this day, it is something I reflect on to redirect me when I feel unmoored, and center me when I am struggling under the weight of endless to-do's.

How do I make my life an act of worship?

The question is confounding in its simplicity. What is worship anyway? The Romans 12 verses connects worship with our bodies and our minds. According to the dictionary, worship as a noun is defined as "the feeling or expression of reverence and adoration for a deity." Boring. The verb form adds a more interesting layer: "to *honor* with religious rites." There it is...Honor. Making my life an act of worship means spending my life honoring Him, with my body as well as my mind.

For so long worship held more of a static, singular meaning. It was just one particular act done in community on one particular day. It was predictable, scripted (literally), and safe. The idea then, that the depth and breadth of my whole life...from the mundane to the exciting...could be an act of worship in its entirety, was and is, provocative.

We spend our days pursuing goals that demand we stay focused, proactive and productive. But worship encourages us to pause and be present...to lift our gaze away from ourselves, unto our Father, and then to those around us. It reframes our perspective, widening our view. It asks us to reexamine our motivations and decisions, drawing us closer to a more nuanced understanding of our world and our relationships. It challenges us to perceive everything and everyone in light of His character. And it beckons us to observe with humility, reflecting His goodness through our interactions with all His other Beloveds. Worship reorients us, and requires the whole of us.

We engage in worship whenever we recognize the Imago Dei in others, choosing to be respectful rather than belittling...whenever we opt to steward our resources, rather than feed our entitlement...when we choose to learn, rather than assume the worst. And of course, we engage in worship whenever we intercede for our hurting neighbors, offer up a skill that benefits our communities, and practice placing boundaries on our time in order to be fully present with whoever is in front of us. Indeed, opportunities for spiritual worship abound. Perhaps the first step is listening...deeply listening, to God and to others, despite how much work we have to do, literally and figuratively. Listening is worship in a way that exhaustion can never be.

Ultimately, worship is not just for God, it is for us.

And we don't just worship with songs of praise.

We worship with our lives, in days.

> *How do you make your life an act of worship? How do you choose to honor Him with your days? I encourage you to examine your resources and relationships and see if you can shift into a more intentional posture of worship. It doesn't need to be a grand gesture. Actually, just the opposite. Join me in trying to cultivate a habit of worship in the small things, and let's see where it leads. And of course, make a note of it somewhere. I pray that Jesus would meet us in these moments and receive our worship with joy.*

reveleena.com

THIRTY-TWO

The Surprising Simplicity of Worship

JACKIE PERSEGHETTI

"As he was drawing near—already on the way down the Mount of Olives—the whole multitude of his disciples began to rejoice and praise God with a loud voice for all the mighty works that they had seen. . .And some of the Pharisees in the crowd said to him, "Teacher, rebuke your disciples." He answered, "I tell you, if these were silent, the very stones would cry out."" —Luke 19:37-40 (ESV)

Her words first smacked me in the face, then rippled across my soul, inviting me to wade into the waters of a paradigm shift. I thought worship had to contain certain components; certainly, worship services did. There's the welcome to ensure everyone feels invited in. Then there's singing to lift emotions, correct perspective, and direct focus. Once focus has been redirected, then the message comes to feed the soul. The stage for worship has been set. Or has it?

As I watched her navigate her Sunday School class of preschoolers, I pondered her words. "Jackie, these little ones experience true worship when they stop -- even if only for a brief second -- and acknowledge God's greatness."

And there it was, plain and simple. No music. No special message. No special timing or circumstance. It was simply acknowledging God's greatness, and it didn't matter if it was only for a brief second, or for several moments. Worship, or "worth-ship," can happen in surprising ways and in surprising circumstances. It can happen in the middle of chaos, or during times of calm sailing. It's not bound by place, rules, regulations, habits, preferences, expectations, or past experiences.

Worship takes your heart into uncharted waters where Jesus gets to be acknowledged as Captain of your ship, fully capable and fully worthy.

And perhaps that's what makes true worship so difficult. We like to be captains at the helm of our own lives. Sometimes we clutch the helm as we're dashed about in storms of life, and other times we hoist the sails, lean on the helm, and become absorbed with a smooth ride. In either case, we have a hard time lifting our eyes from that helm to God's realm. If we aren't careful, worship gets relegated to an event on Sunday mornings -- if even that.

And that is why I love what is recorded in Luke 19:37-40. The very stones would cry out?

Stones need no welcome. They need no music. And they need no message. They are simply there as part of God's creation, designed to express God's glory. How much more then are we, whom God has equipped with a soul to engage in relationship with Himself?

Similar to what goes on in preschoolers, worship of God is not an event; it's an expression of gratitude, awe, and wonder toward God. It isn't scripted or orchestrated, but engaging and personal. It's an intentional choice to stop -- even if only for a brief second -- and acknowledge God's greatness. As surprisingly simple as it is, that's it.

Oh Lord, how my heart longs to be intentional and childlike in my worship of You. Help me to throw off the anchor of tradition that suggests worship should look a certain way or happen at a scheduled time. Lord, you are fully present, fully capable, and fully worthy to be praised. All of Creation points to your glory. Please help my life do the same.

You can find Jackie at www.AKingdomHeartbeat.com and on Instagram and Pinterest.

Free Devotionals and Stories

Want a copy of a Devo Writers Collaboration for free?!

Go to *read.ChristWriters.com*

Subscribe to get:

- a Devo Writers Collaboration ebook
- author interviews and special offers
- invitations to participate however you'd like
  (even voting on new topics and covers)
- links to more free books

Are YOU a writer?

Whether you've never written or you want to grow your author backlist, YOU can join the next collaboration book! Go to DevoWriters.com to learn more.

Check out the Facebook Group, Devo Writers Collaborations to follow along and see how you can contribute:

facebook.com/groups/christiancollections

If you're an author and have any self-publishing needs, contact michael@michaellacey.me.

Last Request

The more reviews, the more readers we can attract. The more readers, the more we can advance the Kingdom and grow the Church in number and depth.

Your help means SO much; please leave an honest review on Amazon!

Thank you!

Made in the USA
Columbia, SC
19 December 2021